ISBN: 979-8-218-95583-0

BORN IN A CHICKEN COOP

John E. Johnson

TABLE OF CONTENTS

BORN IN A CHICKEN COOP

PROLOGUE

The flight from San Francisco down to the Fiji Islands had just landed in Nadi after ten and a half seemingly endless hours over the Pacific. While the three best friends had chatted briefly about Gena's *outrageous* claim as they waited to board the plane at SFO, their seating assignments had them scattered throughout the plane, so any continued conversation about the subject was postponed until their week-long holiday in the South Pacific got fully underway. Besides, they each intended to sleep with earbuds in place during much of the flight. At least Gena certainly did, so that conversation was now on temporary hold.

Carla had vacationed in the islands some four years earlier with her then-husband, Michael, so she firmly insisted that she knew the best spot to experience not only the fabulous island food but also the exciting nightlife that the place offered and directed the cab driver to head straight to Cloud 9.

Over glasses of chilled Chardonnay and small finger sandwiches with exotic fruit slices on the side along with smooth jazz served up by the disc jockey, the subject resurfaced. It was Meg who spoke. Looking at Gena over the top of her fashionable glasses that always seemed to slide down her nose, she simply asked, "Now how am I supposed to believe that you were born in some barnyard or wherever you claim it was. Huh? And this whole thing took place *where?* In New Mexico?"

"Yes! I was born in Roswell, New Mexico. Surely you guys have heard all about Roswell, haven't you? You know, The Roswell Incident and all."

Both girls gave a slight nod, but their faces revealed that their knowledge of the reports from way back in 1947 was vague at best.

Gena continued, "So my big brother, John, the one who is exactly ten years older than I am, just this year said that it wasn't exactly true. But how dare he say such a thing! I've known this to be true my entire life! I was born in a chicken coop!"

By this point Carla was only partially engaged with her two girlfriends at their table since she had been intermittently staring over at an adjoining table for some time now where three guys were lifting bottles of beer in toast after toast to something or someone. She did manage to rejoin the conversation ever-so-briefly by asking, "Why would your brother say that it wasn't true?"

"Oh, he is *great* at telling tall tales. You really won't believe what else he says!"

Meg wanted to know all about this next outlandish claim that Gena was about to reveal, but a beautiful modern jazz tune from saxophonist Boney James had just ended. It had immediately been followed by a louder and faster rhythm and blues number that had completely electrified the dance floor, so Gena was forced to respond loudly and hurriedly:

"Well, listen, he *claims* that he was born exactly nine months after those space aliens crash-landed at that ranch northwest of Roswell near the area where my family lived at the time. Ha! But that's *his* story. He'll have to tell that one. And my story about being born in that chicken coop—it needs to wait. I can tell you all about it later. Let's enjoy this music right now."

Quite suddenly all three of the men at the next table stood and shuffled around for a few moments as if in hesitation about something. They were blond-haired and tanned and fit and appeared to be Aussies. Sizing them up, Gena said of the shortest one, "Now *that's* my kind of stud muffin!"

Just as suddenly, together, they approached the girls and asked, in their thick Australian accents with their right hands extended, if they would like to "have a dance" with them? And without the slightest trace of hesitation, the vacationing American women rose to join them, with Gena making sure to take the hand of her favorite, brown-eyed Aussie!

1 BEANS AND CORNBREAD

Our mother had never been away from the family by herself before, at least not that any of us kids would have been old enough to even know about, and the whole thing just seemed very weird. We were left at home to be taken care of by Daddy alone, which was so incredibly strange. He didn't cook. How would we have anything at all to eat come each suppertime? What, exactly, would we kids manage to scrounge up for ourselves to eat?

No, he never really cooked, unless a large pot of pinto beans counted for cooking, because that he *would* do by performing the Saturday morning ritual where he would sit at the old wooden kitchen table and sort through the mound of pinto beans, that ritual that always seemed to produce a few tiny rocks mixed in with the raw beans. He would then soak them awhile in a big pot before adding tons of salt and additional water and occasionally, if we were very fortunate, a smoked ham hock would make it into the pot. He would then cook the beans for hours and hours on the flat top of the wood-burning monkey stove.

So, at least we would have beans to eat for the week ahead, but who would make the cornbread? It was rather certain that he would not really have much of a clue about how to make the pan of bread for baking in that small portable oven that would sit right on top of the hot wood stove. With any luck, though, Gladys, our big sister of thirteen, would remember enough about Momma's recipe to whip up a few batches as the week went by.

Momma, who was expecting another baby around November that none of us kids realized, had boarded a Trailways bus that was headed up into Kansas on a Friday morning in August for a total of ten days away from the family to visit with our oldest sister, Gwen, who was already married and living with Joe in the little town of Pratt.

We had all viewed the two pictures found in a letter that had been sent home some months earlier of each of them standing individually beside their new green two-toned Chevrolet Biscayne, a nice looking 1953 model, with their trailer home depicted in the background. In the photograph Gwen wore a sweet smile while holding large, white-framed sunglasses and sporting a sleeveless floral print sundress. The picture of Joe revealed a fresh image of youth and rightful pride in the new vehicle.

Each of us wondered what the three of them would be doing up in Kansas during the week of Momma's vacation while we who remained had to endure the extreme heat and blowing dust at home at our place in New Mexico on the outskirts of Roswell, out on the westside just a mile short of what was known as Six Mile Hill.

A one-room dwelling was what we called home with its hard-packed dirt flooring and no running water or electricity. It only had two windows for letting in any daylight—one that was of regular size installed above the oil-cloth-covered kitchen counter in the corner on the south wall and another smaller one that had been placed sideways above our parent's headboard that could be opened for ventilation and allowed late afternoon sunlight to shine in from the west.

Through this elevated window both Little Sister and I had looked out onto the overnight blanket of deep fallen snow on that early morning two years earlier in 1955. To gain that view, we had stood on the front of the mattress up by the pillows, while Gladys and David had positioned themselves directly behind us on the mattress and had wonderfully harmonized,

"Good King Wenceslas looked out, On the Feast of Stephen, When the snow lay round about, Deep and crisp and even."

Our view of the layered snow through that window, accompanied by the lyrics of the song being sung in our ears, served to forever cement a mental image of what the fabled monarch encountered on his frosty nighttime trek across fields of deep snow, fields that now, with early morning sunlight, sparkled under our captivated gaze.

Two years later, in summertime with no school bus to catch, we kids would pass each summer day the same way we always did, with Gladys reading a novel borrowed from the school library and Gloria playing house with her doll. My brother and I would be found outside on the shady side of the house playing with our little toy vehicles on roads carved into the dirt that led to the farmyards with houses, corrals, and barns made from scraps of wood left over from the construction of the place that Daddy had built for his family to live in.

Barefoot and shirtless and wearing faded shorts, we boys would squat for hours on end pretending to be farmers as we drove on the designated roads of our neighboring layouts. While David, being almost a full three years older than I, always seemed to have the much more organized farm with straight fence lines and smoother roads with nicer houses and barns, he *had* let me have the better of the only two toy trucks we possessed. Mine was a plastic royal blue pickup with wheels that actually rolled and a bed for hauling tiny rocks and sand, while his was a cross between red and brown and somewhat smaller in size.

Occasionally our yard dog, Tip, would trapse through our spreads and essentially destroy our carefully laid out farmlands. This full destruction usually occurred during the night while he was nosing around, but we always made a determined effort to turn and pet him just as soon as he came around for a daytime visit. This quick action on our part usually prevented the need for a complete rebuild.

We would spend endless hours playing in the dirt this way. It was only the call from one of our sisters that it was dinnertime or suppertime that would interrupt this play.

And, inevitably, there would not be any surprise on the menu. None whatsoever. We would fill our bowls up to the brim with piping hot pinto beans and grab a wedge or two of cornbread on the side!

2   TARGET PRACTICE

It was a rather typical late Saturday evening out on the Johnson place west of Roswell. The chickens had already roosted just before the sun had finally gone down and darkness had now descended all around. Inside, the kerosene lamp centered on the kitchen table was turned up high to illuminate the small, one-room house.

Even though it was still summer with temperatures to match, the small monkey stove was kept ablaze just enough to keep the full tea kettle hot for the weekly Saturday night baths that each of the four Johnson kids had to endure. The girls were first, one at a time, as they sat on one of the wooden kitchen chairs behind an improvised curtain with feet resting in the large round galvanized tub of water and wash, or, as our Momma called it, "sponge bathe," with a clean individual washcloth. We boys followed, using the same tub of water that had been rewarmed by hot water from the tea kettle.

Oh, how I loathed Saturday nights for this reason! It *was* possible, I supposed, that my two sisters really did prefer to be clean once a week, but I detested the whole process and deeply questioned the necessity of such a ritual in the first place. Besides, who really needed to suffer through the humiliation of sitting naked on that wooden chair, anyway? Maybe Gladys and Little Sister would sneak peeks around the sheet curtain trying to catch a glimpse of me, just like I tried to do when *they* were bathing. But somehow, to my way of thinking, *their* peeking just didn't seem all that fair! It just wasn't right, somehow.

But this Saturday night was not all that typical, really. Momma was still away in Kansas and wouldn't arrive back at the house until the following day when the Trailways bus would pull into the station at around a quarter of five on Sunday afternoon. We kids were anxiously awaiting her return for many reasons, not the least of which was the upcoming break from the monotonous meals, suppertime meals of beans and cornbread with nothing else at all.

She would be happy to see us as well. And she would really appreciate how clean we all were for the week ahead.

The loud pop from the rifle was simultaneous with the crash of the bullet into the wooden casing around the kitchen window. We all jumped, including Daddy, but only he knew what that extremely loud noise had been. He instantly sprang into action by crouching down to our level where we kids were all sitting in our clean pajamas on the ragged couch that rested against the east wall between and the monkey stove and the kitchen counter underneath that window.

He warned us to "Stay down!" We then watched as he crawled on his hands and knees around the metal bathtub on the floor until he got to the table, where he reached up and over to the lit kerosene lamp and turned the flame regulator knob all the way down, plunging the house into darkness.

Gloria had already started sobbing. I was as terrified as everyone else. But it was witnessing our father in a frightened state that made our sense of terror so much stronger. He then repeated himself by saying "Just stay down!" But this time he had whispered it, which only added to the fear we kids were feeling.

Daddy had now lifted a kitchen chair for placement directly in front of his children as we huddled tightly together on the ancient couch in the darkness of the house, a nearly complete darkness that only allowed the faintest silhouette of objects and persons in our immediate area. He then declared, in a rather loud whisper, that he needed Little Sister to stop all that crying. He said that we all needed to be completely silent.

The waiting for yet another rock or whatever kind of projectile it had been to come crashing against the house was maddening. We feared that the next one could come at any moment and would most likely hit the window and shatter the glass, sending shards all over the counter and floor at that end of the room. And any breaking of that glass would probably knock the bright red geranium that Daddy had planted in an old Folgers Coffee can from its special place up on the window ledge.

Daddy knew what had crashed up against the house. He was certain it had been a bullet, and his anguish was centered around the knowledge that someone had already taken direct aim at the window that had been illuminated in the darkness by the lamp light as it flickered against the simple cotton curtain that was drawn closed at the window. Someone had meant us very real harm, and it probably wasn't over yet. For him, the waiting was agonizing. He feared that the next bullet could hit momentarily.

It has long been said that sound travels best at night. Maybe Daddy was counting on that to be true as he sat with his head tilted over to the right and listened for any sound, any sound whatsoever other than the barking from Tip, the dog who had instantly reacted to the blast against the house over on the south side. But he had now stopped what had been incessant barking and was only intermittently growling in the general direction that the rifle shot had likely come from. But Daddy's ears were still straining for the sound of footsteps outside in the yard or the sound of vehicle tires moving across the ground.

Aside from the distinct sound of our heavy breathing and the occasional single sob that escaped from Little Sister, the house was quiet, so totally quiet that we were able to hear the low growls coming from Tip. The very fact that he was even growling at all only increased our terror. *Who* was out there? Was this person trying to hide in the dark from our dog who could sense a presence somewhere out to the south of our place?

Suddenly the stillness was shattered by two very loud pops. Daddy immediately dove off his chair and onto his knees before the couch with his arms stretched to each end in an automatic response of protection for us as we all screamed in fear.

Nothing had slammed up against the house this time, but extremely loud pings had instantly been heard from something that had crashed against the rusty corrugated metal that made up the side walls of the chicken coop out in the north yard. The roosting hens had awakened with a start and were all squawking. And that blasted rooster started crowing repeatedly, with his screeching probably meant as retaliation for the disturbance out at his harem.

Tip was at it once again with his excited barking. He seemed to be frantically running back and forth from the chicken coop to the porch and then around the pickup parked at the south side of the house before charging back again toward the chickens on the north end of the property. He was doing his best to make sense out of the noise and chaos of this direct attack on the property and family that he was desperately trying to protect.

We kids remained tightly cuddled on the couch, but our father had returned to a sitting position in the chair that faced us after he was certain that none of us had been hurt in any way. Never one for making conversation with his children, his silence while we all sat in the near blackness inside the house did not seem out of place at all. Extremely awkward, yes, but who could even focus on that when what had always been our safe environment was now being assaulted this way. Besides, all of us were under a strict silence mandate anyway. It was unfortunate that Tip wasn't under the same demand for silence since his barking was only adding to our sense of fear and impending doom.

It was painstakingly gradual, but our dog had finally stopped running back and forth across the property. It sounded like he had now settled at the southern edge of our lot, out beyond the shed and outhouse, out where a shallow gully ran in from the vacant land just west of us. His barking was no longer frantic but seemingly delivered toward the south of our place, an area with a few scattered houses but one that was in a direct line with ours and slightly more than a half mile away.

When we first heard the sounds, we were startled. The noise seemed to be coming from a place close to our house. It was the sound of boisterous laughter filtering down our way between bursts of barking from Tip. And voices, loud voices, were coming from that direction too, from somewhere just south of us, from what was most likely that rundown Moritsky shack, the place where those three rowdy teenaged boys lived, the same delinquent boys who had long dominated that part of Auto Route West outside of Roswell.

Yes, that had to be the source of the loud talk and laughter. Drunken talk and laughter. It was all coming from that awful Moritsky clan.

We were pretty sure that the out-of-control drinkers were working their way down toward us. I just knew that they were, and I was terrified. My siblings were most likely dreading the very same thing. But Daddy had something else entirely on his mind, apparently. He quickly rose from his chair and headed toward the door. Turning toward us, he told us to just sit still and wait for him to come back. He then quietly opened the door and stepped out into the darkness, quickly closing the door behind him.

Gloria immediately started crying once again, and I certainly felt like letting all my pent-up fear loose, too. But trying very hard to be as brave as David, I held my crying in check. Gladys tried to calm Gloria down enough for her to stop crying, to at least stop crying so loudly, and it finally did work. There was quiet once again inside the house.

Outside, Tip was still frustrated with the drunks down at the Moritsky place. But inside the darkened house, in the hush that had returned, we each heard them, the unmistakable sound of heavy footsteps passing outside right underneath that kitchen window! We gasped and started shivering. Then we heard them again, but this time the movement stopped at the window for a few long moments before moving away in the opposite direction. We were immobilized with bone-chilling fear. Somebody was there in our yard! Somebody had been lurking underneath the kitchen window! There had been no question about it!

Suddenly the door opened, and Daddy stepped in and rapidly closed the door behind him. In a voice no louder than a whisper he said, "Now, Gladys, you're in charge here. I want you to lock this door as soon as I leave. Do not unlock it for anyone while I'm gone. Do you understand? And do not light the lamp. Keep it dark in here. I'm going into town to get the Sheriff."

He then abruptly turned and walked back out into the dark night.

Now Little Sister started in with a wail loud enough to wake the dead!

After Gladys had managed to sidestep the big wash basin in the middle of the kitchen floor and stumble in the darkness over to secure the latch on the door, she proclaimed in the most grown-up voice she could muster, "We still need silence in here! Right now!"

The wailing soon turned to only a whimper as Gladys found her way back to the couch to cuddle up right next to Gloria. As the oldest, she managed to whisper words of comfort and encouragement to each of us, including herself, stating that the footsteps under the window that had so terrified us had been Daddy's all along. But David was having none of it. None. He had retreated into a silent stoic, it seemed, and refused to participate in any whispered assurances that we would be safe until the Sheriff and Daddy arrived.

As for me, I was trembling inside, totally convinced that the immediate need for the Sheriff proved that this long night of terror was just as dangerous as it seemed.

We all heard the motor in the old Chevrolet pickup struggle to a start. And we all noted that Daddy had not switched on the headlights or the running lights as he drove away from the house, since no moving reflection of light came through either of the window curtains. He was still using a great deal of caution as he began his getaway into town. This only served to heighten our fears.

While the distance into town to the Sheriff's office was only about five miles, the entire process seemed to take too long. To the four of us locked away in the dark house, with those Moritsky drunks south of us still carrying on in a frightening manner, the waiting for our father to return was taking forever. We each no doubt wondered how much more of this tension we could stand.

Then we all heard it—the unmistakable squeaking of dry hinges on the screen door as it was slowly being opened! What followed was a hard rapping on the door that caused us to jump out of our skins. And a second, extremely loud knock sent us all into total shock.

"Sheriff Barnett here. You can open up!"

It was only when we heard Daddy's voice telling the Sheriff that we were probably too scared to open the door that we knew with certainty that it wasn't one of those Moritskys trying to get in. It was only then that Gladys rose to make her way to unlock the door.

The Sheriff's bright flashlight lingered on our sister's face which temporarily blinded her. He then swung the beam onto each of our scared faces and asked in a surprisingly soft tone if we were all okay. Each of us nodded sheepishly. Satisfied, he turned toward our father and instructed him to turn on the house lights, smiling broadly as he watched the process unfold for getting the kerosene lamp lit to illuminate the little one-room house.

There was genuine kindness showing in his eyes and his voice sounded so calm and reassuring. I decided that I liked this big, uniformed man with the pistol at his side. And I was sure I liked him even more when he declared that he would head over in his squad car to deal with those drunks who had been shooting off their guns in target practice to torment and endanger their neighbors. He then stated, "Enough is enough!"

Now, finally, this terrible night was coming to an end.

3 ON THE NORTH WIND

"It's just way too cold out here! We're going to freeze to death!"

"Why do we have to stay out here where it's so cold, anyway? How come Gladys gets to stay in the house where it's warm? That's not fair! It's just not fair!"

The complaints originating from Johnny, a shivering nine-year-old, and the questions that followed from eight-year-old Gloria were not directed at anyone, but our older brother, David, at twelve, had probably offered some workable answers as he sat beside us outside in the forty-degree temperature made colder by an icy wind coming all the way down from off the Rockies way up north. It was the next-to-last day in November, so naturally it was cold that early in the morning.

We were huddled together on an assortment of long sections of scrap lumber that had been stacked up against the sunny side of Daddy's handmade shed, a primitive enclosure with only three walls serving as nothing more than a chicken coop to accommodate one ornery rooster and six rather scrawny Leghorn hens. The birds seemed completely oblivious to the weather as they clucked and pecked around on the bare windswept ground just outside the shed even though their feathers kept getting lifted by the wind. They seemed equally uninterested in the dark blood-stained ground beside the chopping block that had been used just the morning before to behead one of their sisters for an upcoming afternoon feast.

We, however, were ready for immediate relief from the bone-chilling wind and cold. By the height of the winter sun, it seemed to be approaching noontime, probably, but the temperature had barely risen at all. If it hadn't been for our preoccupation with the cold, we might have realized that it was about time for our dinner. And had we even been able to remember it, the meal would have included a touch of leftovers from the meager Thanksgiving spread that the family had enjoyed only the day before. There would likely be some of the canned jellied cranberry sauce left, and maybe a small amount of cornbread stuffing and thin, greasy gravy to go along with whatever might be left of the dark meat from the small hen that had been substituted for our turkey dinner. But the only thing we children could concentrate on this morning was surviving outside in the bitter November cold.

The shut-out from the warm house had begun just after our breakfast of oatmeal mush around eight-thirty that morning. Without any explanation at all, we children had been informed that we needed to stay outside until further notice. Not one of us dared to question the firm directive from our father, since children were always to be seen and not heard. This ironclad rule could never be deviated from, nor could it ever even be questioned. There was never any free and open conversation with Daddy, anyway.

We had called out to our big sister, Gladys, on the two occasions when she'd stepped out of the house and headed over to the cistern some five yards from the porch to pull up clean water into the communal drinking bucket before letting the screen door slam on her way back inside the house. Her only reply to us, both times, had been an admonishment to "Just hush" and wait until it was time for us to come inside. She said that she would let us know just as soon as that time came.

"What's really going on in there?" My question was no doubt shared by each of us as we wondered why so much fresh water was being used and why Daddy had stood on the small porch and tossed wastewater onto the sloped ground on the three occasions when he'd opened the door. He had glanced over in our direction as we shivered in the cold next to the shed, but no real eye contact had been made and nothing was said to us. He had seemed preoccupied, and his movements seemed a bit rushed. And he, too, let the screen door slam shut as he reentered the house. We found that to be more than a little strange, since a usual source of real agitation for him was hearing the slamming of any door. Ever.

We each had heard our mother cry out once the first time Gladys was still closing the door behind her with the overfilled bucket of sloshing water gripped in her hand. We had heard the same muffled noise coming from inside the house a couple of times afterwards. Maybe our parents were arguing again. There was nothing new there. But we couldn't help but wonder if this fighting was about the three of us, the three young children banished to the outside on this cold November morning.

"All right. You can come in the house now!"

It was the loud voice of our sister who was standing by the opened screen door. She stepped back inside as we three took off in a fast run seeking the heat that the pot-bellied stove would be putting out.

As we crossed the threshold from the wooden porch and stepped down to the hard-packed dirt floor of the dwelling, we each heard the unfamiliar sound of soft gurgling coming from our parent's bed over in the corner where our mother was propped up with several pillows and holding a small blanket wrapped around something. Could it be a brand-new baby? Momma appeared exhausted but still managed to smile as we crowded around to get our first look at this tiny infant. It was Gladys who spoke first, telling us that it was a girl who had weighed in at exactly ten pounds and that her name was Geneva. Geneva Gay Johnson.

Our father stood over by the monkey stove. His face appeared flushed, and he wore a sheepish grin as he watched all of us make much of the baby he had just delivered—the little girl who blinked back at us with her dark eyes. And what a perfect and tiny nose on that pink face! Her occasional cooing was music to our ears. Could it be that she was really trying to communicate with us? Surely, she somehow knew that her siblings smiling down at her were completely in love with her, instantly in love with this precious bundle of new life.

Finally, our mother said that it was probably time for the baby to take a nap, too, since that was what she fully intended to do. We reluctantly backed away and scooted over to the couch to chatter about this new member of our family—the total surprise that had been added to the list of daughters that had names starting with the letter "G" accompanied by a middle name for each sister that rhymed: Gwendolyn Kay, Gladys May, Gloria Fay, and now Geneva Gay. We all endorsed this naming pattern as cute and unique if not somewhat quirky as well.

So *that* was what had forced the three of us to stay outside the whole morning in freezing cold weather! Somehow, in some unknown but obviously fantastic fashion, a new member of our family had magically arrived. Neither Little Sister nor I had the slightest clue how it had happened. If our brother David knew, he had certainly kept it all to himself.

Perhaps little Geneva had come in on that persistent north wind that was still blowing outside, somehow carried into the house by a big white stork. Everyone already knew all about big storks that carried a baby-blanket hanging from its beak. But just how did we manage to miss seeing it arrive? And how did that even make any real sense? It was such a mystery, and not a single person who was really "in the know" was saying anything.

And Momma had not been saying anything, either. Not a word. None of her children even knew that she was "expecting." She had not said anything about it, and no one had any suspicion whatsoever, since her large abdomen had not really appeared any different than always before.

Yes, the delivery of this little baby girl named Geneva absolutely had to have been by a big white stork that had found our place in Roswell, New Mexico and had flown right into the house. At least that mystery was finally solved!

4 "CAN'T WE JUST GET THIS DEAL DONE?"

We watched as the big, light gray Ford truck slowly rolled to a stop at the northwest corner of the house. The driver's door squeaked open to reveal a heavyset Caucasian man in his fifties, most likely, who called out with a loud "Hello" as he waved to all four of us barefoot kids clustered together and gawking at the scene unfolding right before us. From a safe distance behind the truck, we slinked around toward the right side to catch a glimpse of the passenger sliding down onto the wide running board where she waited for the man to help her down to the ground. After seeing the short Hispanic woman, we all took off in a run for the house to tell our parents that "some buyers" had pulled up to trade their truck for our house.

After we all emerged from the house to stand out in the barren dirt yard, the buyer approached with the woman in tow and thrust out his calloused right hand to shake Daddy's hand, which he pumped repeatedly as he loudly proclaimed,

"My name is William Reed, but everybody just calls me Billy, 'ya know. This here's my wife, Marina. She don't speak English too good."

There was a rather awkward return of greeting from Daddy, but our mother instantly bristled and deeply frowned when Marina greeted her in Spanish with an "Hola, como esta?" We all knew how much Momma loathed being mistaken for being of Mexican descent herself just because of her dark hair and dark, deeply suntanned face and arms—and it had just happened to her again! Momma did somehow manage to give a toothy grin, though, and quickly invited the couple to join them inside to check out the house that was for sale while telling her children to remain outside.

Now we had an excellent opportunity to investigate everything about that old Ford truck while the adults were busy inside the house! We felt a real urgency to start checking it out, since enormous thunderheads were forming out west and quickly heading our way.

Gladys and Little Sister weren't interested in the big truck anymore and headed off to the small doorless shed out near the path to the outhouse to sit on the old mattress on the floor, where Gladys immediately opened her unfinished Nancy Drew book while Gloria played dress up with her little doll.

But David and I proceeded with our inspection. First, we marveled at the dual rear wheels and big tires. At twenty inches, they seemed so enormous! We then stepped up onto the running board on the driver's side, peering into the cab through the open window to see the smooth bench seat and the rectangular instrument gauge cluster on the dashboard. A strong odor of stale cigarettes from the nearly overflowing ashtray assaulted us, but that was unimportant, since our real mission was to check the odometer reading. David was tall enough to lean into the cab. He quickly announced that the recorded miles were 89,183. We both immediately realized that the truck was already nearing its last gasp, since vehicles that managed to reach fifty thousand miles or more during the 1950s were practically ready for the nearest scrapyard.

Using the running board as a ladder, we then scaled up to walk around on the vast surface of the flatbed, realizing that any camper built on it would be gigantic and by far the largest one that Daddy had ever built.

Jumping down to the ground, we then proceeded to check under the front end for any signs of a telltale oil or transmission or brake fluid leak, which was a necessary part of any real examination by two young sleuths. Finding only windswept ground without any stains, we emerged from underneath the truck just as the adults were walking toward the one-and-a-half-ton truck. We overheard Billy loudly bragging to Daddy about the full one hundred horsepower of the flathead V8 engine with its ability to easily pull "just about anything."

And now it was Daddy's turn to evaluate the truck. David and I kept silent as we watched him climb up into the cab and look all around inside, first at the floorboard and then over at that nasty ashtray. After he had studied the dashboard gauges, he turned to address Billy who was standing on the ground next to the open truck door. His only question as he stepped onto the warped running board to exit the cab was, "How many miles are on this engine?"

"How many miles? Oh, there's only around seventy thousand as I can recollect. Now I'm just the second owner, 'ya know, but it's dead certain that the few miles I've put on this here truck have only been real easy ones," he responded while resting his hand on the dented left front fender before moving to the grill to open the hood. "Nope. I never really hauled much of anything with this here rig. She's really a beauty!"

We all heard the distinct clicking of Daddy's tongue against his teeth. We knew that this generally meant that he was pretty much irritated with something. By our best guess, he had already had enough of Billy's blustering if not outright lying about the nearly worn-out Ford truck.

We could only guess at what outrageous things he might have said while inside our house as he walked about deciding if the little dwelling would be *suitable* for Marina and himself to trade their truck and a little cash for. We were by now pretty sure that anything he had said or asked was less than complimentary at best and likely absolutely demeaning to our parents.

Meanwhile, as Daddy leaned over to peer down onto the Ford engine while standing on the narrow front bumper, the ladies stood by without speaking. Both were intently listening to the loud rumble of thunder from the approaching storm that would certainly be a real cloudburst before very much longer.

Why was the examination of the motor that Billy had started up so incredibly brief? We boys surely knew. Daddy had already endured enough of this proposed trade for his house, the place that he had built from scratch with his own hands. No. His mind was already made up. Ole Billy Boy was *not* going to be successful.

All remaining inspections were only perfunctory. He did the obligatory kicking of one of the dual, nearly bald tires at the back, after which he squinted down to read the size of the tire and then stepped back a few feet to size up the enormity of the wheel itself. We boys knew that he was mentally evaluating just how in the world he would ever be able to even break the bead on one of those tires when it came time for changing a flat and making patches to the innertube. And how much incredible energy would be required to pump such a huge tire back up with only the hand air pump kept in the tire repair box?

Billy had decided to remain quiet during these last items of inspection. Was he finally getting a clue that this deal was falling apart? He just stood back behind Daddy as he went through all the motions that were intended to look like a thorough and honest appraisal of the enormous truck.

When Daddy motioned for his wife to join him over by the truck door, the first clap of thunder let loose, startling everyone. Momma then reluctantly walked over toward the cab to perform the very last item of inspection that our father was performing. He asked our mother to step up onto the truck's running board while using the door frame for support. And perhaps in what was not a surprise to those of us watching, and especially to Marina, not even the tip of her shoe managed to contact the running board as she raised her leg while revealing her thigh-length hosiery that had a tight roll just below the knee.

By this point Momma was thoroughly disgusted and longed for this whole thing to be over and done with. She was pretty much mortified by this display for all to see. And just then a threatening clap of thunder broke loose directly overhead.

Only moments later, a loud wail was heard coming through the screen door of the house. The baby, six-month old Geneva, had been startled awake and was wondering where everyone else was. Her wailing cry was persistent, and this was Momma's escape bell. Off she scurried toward the crying baby.

Apparently sensing the need to act quickly, both to erase the image of our mother's inability to access entry into the truck and to beat the impending rain, Billy thrust out two crisp bills, one hundred dollars each, stating, "Here's two hundred dollars cash and this nice truck here in trade for yer place. What do you say to that?"

Daddy's reply was quick, too, as he simply said, "The cash price for the house is four hundred dollars and a trade for a pickup that I can use. I am not interested in a big ton and a half flatbed truck. Not interested at all. So, no. We have no deal, Mr. Reed."

Billy pulled out a third big bill and implored, "Can't we just get this deal done?"

The first drops of rain were now hitting the ground all around and making little craters in the fine dust. Just a minute or two more and a real deluge would let loose.

"No, sir. We do *not* have a deal here, but I do wish good luck to you and your wife in your search for a suitable house out this way."

Billy was now red-faced and appeared angry as he motioned for Marina to come to the truck, where he lifted her up onto the running board and she climbed into the cab and slid under the steering wheel and across to the passenger side. Without looking back at all, he gunned that old Ford V8 and wheeled around to the right.

The hard downpour was now getting us soaked as we monitored their departure from our wet yard, but my brother and I weren't finished watching just yet.

We saw the heavy flatbed truck make tracks in the fast-forming mud while spewing out billows of blue exhaust smoke as Billy hastily shifted through all the gears.

Daddy had already dashed into the house to escape the cloudburst, so he missed seeing the evidence of the failing motor in that old Ford truck. But David and I had most certainly observed it.

And we had also been witnesses to something else, something that made us instantly and deeply proud of our father. He had finally won at something, and this time it would probably not be remembered as a bad "horse trade" that would ultimately result in any loss. No. Not this time!

We had witnessed one failed business transaction, a potential deal that had utterly fallen apart—at least for Billy and Marina Reed, anyway!

5   THE CALL OF THE OZARKS

Everything about the move from New Mexico to the Ozarks during the latter part of that summer in 1958 was joyously celebrated by all the Johnson kids. This time we were really leaving for good, not just for a week or so in the summer as we'd done in previous years when, on a June afternoon on the very last day of school, we would leave the schoolyard behind us to journey in our gypsy-looking pickup and trailer and begin the first leg of the sojourn.

The trip always took every bit of a full week, since hours-long afternoon stops were made in little towns along the route in Texas and Oklahoma for the door-to-door potholder and apron peddling that we kids performed to keep gasoline in the truck gas tank and spongy round-topped white bread, jarred Sandwich Spread, and cold cuts like souse and bologna in our stomachs.

But this time wasn't exactly the same. This was a full-blown move far away from the place that Daddy had always said was nothing more than a God-forsaken, wind-blown desert.

All our essential household belongings were packed away inside a homemade Masonite-sided trailer that was painted in glossy white with a dark olive-green canvas tightly stretched across the top and anchored down with white rope pulled through the grommets and firmly tied to long nails that protruded from the wooden trailer box. The chassis had no springs and employed a trailer tongue fashioned from a ten-foot-long section of lumber that measured a mere six-by-six inches in diameter with a standard two-inch ball hitch bolted onto the end.

The tightly packed belongings stowed in the trailer included Momma's treasured Singer sewing machine and two kerosene lamps with their spare chimneys. Cooking equipment like a cast iron skillet and the pot for cooking pinto beans was kept separately in a large cardboard box and placed just inside the back of the pickup bed for easy access every evening around four PM when we would stop and make camp alongside the two-lane highways on the summer sojourn to our intended Missouri destination.

Our parents obviously felt the same joy that we kids did. A look of genuine relief coupled with a sense of adventure brightened their faces as they loaded the pickup and trailer for the journey. This was intended to be one more brand-new beginning, and they were clearly relishing all of it.

(Any true retrospective review of this move, though, decades later, would prove that it was yet another in a series of "horse-trading" moves that only managed to exchange one set of enormous problems for a load of different ones, something like running away and not bothering to look behind for any reason).

But the Johnsons couldn't see that far ahead as the unsightly truck with its ragged trailer slowly pulled away from the small house that Daddy had single-handedly built during the early spring of 1953. The place had served as our home for nearly five years and had been the birthplace of the newest member of our family, baby Geneva.

The one-room dwelling with its two windows, pot-bellied wood stove and hard-packed dirt floor would now be inhabited by someone entirely different. The elderly couple had just wanted a small house where they could live out whatever remaining years they had while drawing their ever-so-meager retirement check that arrived in the mailbox up on the highway every month from the Social Security Administration. And the Johnson place had seemed perfect to them.

Flush with four hundred dollars in cash stuffed deep into Momma's purse and a decrepit Chevrolet pickup with an inline 6-cylinder engine that was still in fairly good running condition despite a radiator that had a real tendency to boil over after long uphill climbs, our parents were looking ahead to the rolling hills of the Ozarks and yet another brand new opportunity to set up housekeeping some six hundred and seventy-five miles east of Roswell in a true promised land of "milk and honey," a land with abundant water everywhere and absolutely no maddening dust storms.

That's what the Ozarks did. They called and just kept calling, and Gene and Harleigh Johnson were always listening. And they had no resistance to this magnetic pull. Besides, practically anywhere pointed to on any roadmap would be preferable to the Llano Estacado, the stacked plains of eastern New Mexico.

No, there was seemingly no valid reason to look back toward Roswell and our humble dwelling place that slowly drifted out of our sight behind us. Instead, the entire family was completely focused on those pretty green hills up ahead.

Even little Geneva, at seven months old, sensed the anticipation and real excitement radiating from each of us. And whatever the excitement was all about, it was special and contagious!

Shorty and Eva Robinson had graciously allowed us to camp at the edge of their property for the week when classes had started over at Westview School in Neosho. Although it was a full two miles each way by a dirt road to get to the school campus, the walk was something we could manage, and particularly so on those hot afternoons during that week when Shorty happened along around three o'clock in his ancient black truck and stopped for us to climb up into the bed where we stood clutching onto the wooden side rails with the wind blowing against our faces on the ride out to our borrowed campsite.

Their place was seemingly in the deep woods yet very close to the road. Hardly any trees had been cleared away except where the small shack had been built for their housing.

A wood-burning cookstove had been set up outside in the yard just beyond the door where Eva would do her cooking regardless of the weather for the day. On that first weekend, we children had all witnessed the raindrops falling into the hot skillet of grease where

Eva was frying up some fatty bacon for the breakfast meal that she had invited us Johnsons to share.

Momma was determined at all costs to decline the breakfast invitation, so she instructed their daughter, Delfi, who was approximately Gloria's age, to inform her mother that we had already eaten our cornmeal mush for breakfast and were breaking camp to head over to the small cabin offered by the Waters family, a place that was on the Westview School bus line.

We waved our goodbyes to Shorty and Eva and Delfi and their fifteen-year-old son who were all standing in the small clearing next to Shorty's old truck. From what I could see, it appeared that Delfi was sobbing, already missing her newfound friend, Gloria.

All previous summer trips to the Ozarks, like this one, had always ended on the forty acres belonging to the Clarks from out near Racine, Missouri. We kids would eagerly pile out from the back of the canvas-covered shell over the pickup bed to immediately plop down onto the cool, luxuriously thick green grass under a shade tree to search for four-leaf clovers on the lawn out in front of the two-bedroom log cabin that served as the home for our very special friends, Charles and Virginia Clark, and their three children, Wesley and Zonna and young Mark.

What absolute pleasantness that lawn evoked for us desert dwellers! It was clothed in dappled sunlight under the shade tree and the tiniest breeze created moving patterns across the sought-for clovers that sported a highly elusive fourth leaf. The slanting late afternoon sun illuminated all our faces, producing a dreamlike state, an image of pure tranquility in the Missouri paradise down in the Ozarks.

A green lawn! Dappled shade! Not the bare dirt of treeless desert yards. Paradise instead!

Gladys, the oldest Johnson sibling among us kids, and Zonna, who would join us for the lawn treasure hunt, seemed to always manage to find the most four-leaf clovers. They always did! So, it was a very welcomed interruption when Virginia would invite us inside for ice-cube-filled metal tumblers of Kool-Aide to enable us to cool off and settle down from the long road trip that had just terminated at their welcoming place in the wonderful Ozarks. And what pure refreshment that always was—to sit around inside the cabin with the electric fan in the north window blowing cool air and to just relax with the cold, sugary drinks!

We all found Zonna to be so beautiful with her long, curly auburn hair. She and Gladys were the same age and had become fast friends from spending part of each summer together. This friendship was so special that Zonna even gave up her lower bunk for Gladys to sleep in while borrowing her brother Wesley's top bunk. He was relegated to sleeping out on the back porch which he didn't mind, since it was much like a camp-out to him.

The rest of the Johnsons slept inside the unpainted barn built into the side of a gentle slope out beyond the thriving vegetable garden and the clothesline, a weathered structure with barn doors that opened to the musty but sweet smell of old furniture.

And there was an unbelievable treasure stored inside "Clark's barn" that we all invariably gravitated to: the brown furniture piece that housed the still-working antique wind-up Victrola record player! Stored inside the cabinet were numerous records from the Roaring Twenties, old records in brown paper sleeves with depictions of the various artists in stylistic attire and poses. What an absolute treasure trove of music for us Johnson kids to listen to! But listening was less of a focus for me than angling to be the one who got to perform the hand cranking that allowed the player to come alive. I declared that the winding was "my job!"

But this trip was different. We were unable to stay in the Clark's barn this time since their young toddler, Mark, who was almost three, had come down with a summer cold with bronchitis and then pneumonia. On his doctor's orders, he was to remain essentially isolated until the problem was fully corrected. And the last thing we needed was for Geneva, who wasn't even a year old yet, to catch anything dangerous.

Things were totally safe health-wise, though, over at the Waters' place up next to the highway. Geneva was just starting to walk during that week, but Little Sister preferred to lug her around on her hip as we all spent time outside in the sunshine that Saturday morning. The entire eastern portion of the acreage that faced out to the highway had been cleared, but a significant fringe of hickory saplings had remained intact to serve as a filter to shield the house and all the surrounding equipment and old rusted vehicles from any direct view from the road.

Who even knows where we found the pocketknife? Both girls watched with fascination as we boys took turns carving a complete circle around the trunk of one of the young trees. Geneva seemed to love the texture of the small chunk of bark that I handed her and wrinkled up her little nose at the taste of the wet underside, causing each of us to laugh at her.

And who knows where Daddy had come from? There he stood glaring at the damaged tree trunk. He then circled all around to see the complete five-inch-wide ring of missing bark. David, Gloria, even little Geneva, and I were all beaming at the clever "artwork" that had been carved into the tree trunk. Little Sister then spoke up to ask, "Isn't that so pretty, Daddy?"

Our handiwork had not favorably impressed him! Far from it. But if he had wanted to thoroughly scold or even punish us, he held that anger in check. Instead, he simply informed us that the young tree might now be doomed. He told us that a trunk must be intact for any tree to thrive.

Perhaps he just forgave us right on the spot since he understood that we knew nothing at all about trees and the purpose of bark. After all, we were from the desert. And there really *weren't* any trees out on the desert!

Our quick departure from Missouri was very much like Zorro disappearing in the middle of the night!

While Mrs. Waters had been informed that we would be heading down south into Arkansas at first light on Wednesday morning and had let Virginia Clark know about it, Vera, the Westside School attendance clerk, had not been notified. She was left to wonder where the Johnson students were.

After making the afternoon trek from the school bus drop off point up on the blacktop to her home a mile away, a walk that first headed downhill on the rocky dirt lane before heading back up again to the crest of the long hill where a clearing in the woods off on the right side of the road revealed the square log cabin and a weathered barn, Zonna had immediately called out, "Mother, listen! David wasn't in our class today. And Johnny and Gloria weren't at school either."

Virginia's reply was straightforward. "Yes, I know all about that. Mrs. Waters had her husband drive over here to tell me that they had all just lit out first thing this morning for somewhere down in Arkansas. Only the Good Lord knows where, though!"

6   THE RUNAWAY

The drive down to Mena in western Arkansas from southwest Missouri was an easy five hour run. It was a simple drive that followed Route 59 south until it joined U.S. Route 71 leading down to Ft. Smith before finally reaching our destination in the town of Mena. But our early morning trip down the road had taken double that amount of time since a blowout on the rear tire on the pickup had forced us to stop for the necessary tire repair work. We had only made it a short distance past the town named Siloam Springs, but at least we were already in Arkansas!

An unmounted spare rubber tire was always stashed underneath the triple-thickness plywood bed in the back of the pickup, but gaining access to it required the removal of items that blocked it in. The ordeal of pulling everything out and laying each item along the edge of the road took some time, but the real work that required an hour and sometimes even two was Daddy's repair of the damaged innertube. He would take out the small, tattered cardboard box that held the tools required for vulcanizing and cementing the series of patches onto the tube, using the small iron hand clamp to guarantee that the seals would hold. This task would always be performed while sitting on an upturned wooden crate beside the pickup using the skills that many years of doing the exact same thing had produced. He demonstrated considerable patience during the entire process, as always.

He *had* shouted out the closest thing to a curse that he ever uttered, though. It was his customary, "Well, glory!" that followed that explosive blowout that had sent the truck and trailer careening on that wobbling course to an eventual stop beside the highway. But he had otherwise remained calm and focused as he used the red ratchet-levered hand jack to raise the axle to get the now-ragged tire removed.

After we were rolling once again, Momma spotted a wide pull off that would be totally suitable for setting up our campsite for the night. Even though we had just passed a mileage sign along the highway stating that Mena was only eight miles further ahead, it was already right at four in the afternoon. It was time to get the jarred bacon grease sizzling for frying up the cornmeal mush patties and opening a can of peas for suppertime.

We had finally arrived! No longer in the deep woods of Missouri, we had managed to slowly cripple along the tree-lined highways of Arkansas until the teensy-weensy town of Mena had come into full view.

It was Thursday, and we were now at our new home! We Johnsons, at least the kids, were thrilled beyond our wildest dreams since we would be living right in town in a house with running water. Not real indoor plumbing with a bathroom, mind you, but at least a faucet at the kitchen sink. There would no longer be any need for hauling in water from a cistern or a well or a spring.

In addition to running water out in the kitchen, each room had wooden flooring covered with linoleum. Those two features alone made the house seem like a real mansion to us compared to what we had left behind out in the desert of New Mexico. And even though the white paint on the clapboard siding was faded and the tin roof appeared rusty in places, our house still looked comparable to every other one on the block with only a single exception—the beautiful two-story Queen Anne with its curving wrap-around porch that sat directly across the street. It gleamed from a fresh coat of white paint with light gray trim around the windows and on the steps leading up to the gray wooden planks that covered the porch. Oh, how lavishly rich that Gillian family appeared to be!

I had overheard our parents wondering just how it would be possible to afford, long term, the forty-five dollars in monthly rent for our new residence down at the end of Second Street. I wondered about that too since the amount seemed so outrageously high. But happy that I didn't need to deal with such grown-up things, I walked on through the kitchen and out the rear door to begin my exploration of the jungle that made up the back yard. There was a distinct path that headed west into tall shrubbery before making a bend to the right and then disappearing altogether. Walking along on this trail, I soon ran smack dab into a little outhouse. Retracing my steps, I then explored around to the south of the path where I felt certain that I had heard running water. And to my delight, a little•creek was discovered right alongside the edge of the lot. It was live water. Unbelievable!

Continuing to the front yard, I joined Gloria and baby Geneva who were sitting on the wooden steps of the long front porch. Then I just blurted it out, "There's a real creek right next to us. It's on our property! Come with me and I'll show you."

Even though Geneva had already started to walk, I scooped her up anyway and headed over to the trees and tall brush to get a good look at the meandering creek. Wanting a clearer view, though, that would be unobstructed by the thick brush, we then crossed the grassless front yard and the driveway to the bare dirt street that served our address of 1111 South Second Street. Turning to the right we quickly reached the small concrete bridge that allowed the creek water to travel eastward underneath the roadway. Resting one foot atop the low-rise bridge, I balanced Geneva on my knee for her direct view of the water flowing over the smooth, iron-colored rocks lining the creek bottom. Geneva appeared fascinated with the water and even spoke to us about it in her sweet gibberish. Little Sister and I were certainly fascinated as well. Running water—flowing away to who knew exactly where? It really was unbelievable to previous desert-dwellers like us!

.

"Where's Geneva? It's now past time for her bottle and nap."

Gladys had called out from inside the kitchen before entering the bedroom where I sat thumbing through a well-worn but coveted Superman comic book.

"She's cuddling with her teddy bear on that big rag rug right out there in the living room."

Gladys seemed satisfied with my answer and moved on into the next room. But returning to the bedroom, she stated, "No, she's not out there anymore. Did she come in here?"

We searched on the other side of the bed. We even looked underneath the iron bedstead. Gladys then headed back into the kitchen for a look around out there while scolding me over her left shoulder with a muttered, "You're *supposed* to be watching her!"

Gloria had heard the conversation but knew that the baby wasn't in the back storage room where she was sorting through the clothes that had been unpacked from one of the cardboard moving boxes. She called out to let Gladys know that Geneva was not in that room with her.

"Geneva is missing! I need you guys to get up from whatever you're doing and help find her. Right now! Look everywhere. And I mean look everywhere you can possibly think of!" There was clear frustration in her command and her voice revealed a heavy touch of real panic as well.

David was off on some walking adventure. Momma and Daddy had driven off to locate a grocery store. So only Gloria and I were available to help with the search. And even without the scolding from my big sister, I was nevertheless feeling responsible for the missing girl. I guess it really had been my assignment to babysit her.

Little sister and I joined forces and started by calling Geneva's name throughout each room of the house. We noticed that Gladys had stepped into the back yard and was heading over toward the old crumbling single-car detached garage. We decided to head out the front door and look around on the big porch. We found no little girl. But we did find something lying across the bottom step. It was Geneva's soggy diaper that had clearly fallen off! But where was Geneva?

Geneva was not found on either side of the house. And neither was she found behind any shrubbery or behind the enormous sycamore tree that anchored one side of the short driveway.

So where was she? We stepped into the street and first looked to the north toward Mrs. Embry's yard, then across the street in a catty-cornered direction to the Putman's small house, then directly across to the Gillian wrap-around porch. No Geneva was seen anywhere.

When we turned our eyes to the south, though, there she was!

Leaning over the low bridge abutment at the creek, she was *buck naked* and peering down at the flowing water. We called her name without response. When we yelled out her name, though, she was able to hear over the sound of the gurgling creek and turned her face toward us with a grin plastered all over it. She then stood upright and turned in our direction in all her naked splendor and started to gingerly walk on bare feet toward us!

Could this action by the little runaway toddler on her stolen journey down to the creek portend a lifelong penchant for sojourns and grand adventures? Only time would tell.

7   POTHOLDERS & APRONS

How we Johnsons ended up in Roswell, New Mexico again in the late summer of 1959 after one full year in the Ozarks was anyone's guess. No one could make any real sense out of our sudden departure.

We were leaving the absolute splendor that we had enjoyed down in those pretty green hills of western Arkansas near the Oklahoma state line, down where the little live creek flowed right past our house, that creek where crawdads hid under the smooth rocks of the creek bottom. We had so enjoyed living where we could walk, not just to our school and to church, but to just about any destination in the small town, like to the only drug store right downtown to sit on a swiveling red-topped stool at the soda fountain and enjoy an occasional cherry phosphate, or to wander the wide river-rock-strewn banks of the shallow river that flowed beside the highway leading into town.

We had loved the sound of the soft whistle as the afternoon freight train rumbled through town. We had loved the sound of rainfall on our tin roof as it lulled us to sleep at night. And we had loved, beyond measure, a sense of true neighborliness as we talked with Mrs. Embry about her skills in making lye soap, or played softball with the Putman boy after school in the street filled with the distinct aroma of pinto beans cooking on the stovetop coming from our own kitchen, or visited the Davis family up at their corner house on Saturdays where Butch and Ozella would welcome us inside to watch reruns of something so wonderful, a phenomena we had not experienced before—a moving picture show in black and white of The Lone Ranger and Tonto riding up some trail on the TV set in their living room.

Had our sudden departure from paradise been the result of inflationary pressures on the family? While the short-lived recession of 1958 had not sent overall prices soaring in 1959, had even a small increase in the price of our groceries, kerosene, gasoline, or the water bill been a jolt to an extremely fragile budget that really could not be overcome?

We children had picked up little scraps from a few of the conversations between our parents, but the one tidbit that had meant something was when Momma had said that it was totally customary to experience a rent increase on the anniversary of a lease. Likely it *had* been that ten dollar increase in the rent starting on the first day of September in 1959 that had been a real tipping point, a final obstacle that just seemed insurmountable to Daddy.

Without question, we all knew that funds were tight. They had always been tight as far as anyone could remember. The monthly walk with Daddy to City Hall to accept our allotment of boxed surplus commodity foodstuffs underscored extremely deep poverty. My brother and I earnestly hoped, every single time, that no one we knew would recognize either of us as we carried one boxful each on the journey across town back toward our house way down on Second Street.

We all knew exactly where the monthly income came from. During our first six weeks in Arkansas, the only source of revenue had come through Momma who had worked the evening shift each Thursday through Sunday as the dishwasher down at Joe's Diner until those successive weeks of standing for eight straight hours each shift had taken an awful toll on her forty-nine-year-old body. And, furthermore, she was not at home to cook the meals nor to look after her baby, Geneva, so that source of income really had to stop.

It was then that Gladys came to the rescue. Since she had not returned to school following the move from New Mexico, she exchanged her unpaid babysitting of little Geneva for paid employment caring for the widow Yarborough. The elderly lady required a live-in companion and general caregiver for her wellbeing in the stately home that sat across from Janssen Park. Even though Gladys had to walk down to the family home every Saturday afternoon to deposit her entire weekly cash wages into the family general fund, she still benefitted from the occasional gifts given to her by the elderly patient and certainly from the healthy meals that she prepared for the two of them every day from the quality ingredients she kept on hand in the refrigerator and pantry.

She had described her private living quarters upstairs as being beautifully furnished. A window view of the graceful water fountain in the park served as icing on a cake that represented her Mena lodging away from home.

A determined effort had been made by our mother to generate some additional income from mending and sewing and general alterations as advertised on the sign planted out in the front yard. The Masonite board had been painted white and measured three feet high by about eight feet long. David had ever-so-carefully painted capital letters in black that read,

ALTERATIONS WANTED, followed by smaller letters on the next line that simply stated, INQUIRE WITHIN.

Even though Momma's intentions had certainly been noble, the location of our house down at the bottom of unpaved Second Street, which scarcely ever had any through traffic, and the lack of a telephone made this attempt at commerce almost futile. There were the scattered collections of one dollar and fifty cents from hemming a pair of dress slacks and the quarter or two from replacing missing buttons, but those jobs were so few that it was very disheartening.

David had secured an after-school newspaper route to deliver the regional Mena paper three times every week. However, the cost was exactly two dimes from each subscriber. That weekly take was so dreadfully little that no contribution to the fund was expected, let alone even possible. Besides, he had employees to pay! Both Gloria and I helped throw the papers up onto the porch of each subscriber's house and were compensated with ten cents apiece each week which was sufficient for a long-lasting hard-serve ice cream cone every Saturday afternoon—with a whole nickel left over—from the smiling man behind the walk-up window of his tiny shop down on Mena Street south of the railway station. So, neither Johnny nor Gloria could make any real contribution to the family fund, either.

But now, that dreaded morning had finally arrived. We were leaving! We pulled away from 1111 South Second Street on the third morning of August in the summer of 1959. It was a Monday. Just before ten in the morning, we headed west once again.

Almost seven hundred miles lay ahead as we crossed the state line into Oklahoma. We looked the same as we had just one year earlier, but this time we were heading in the opposite direction in our jalopy pickup with the hideous homemade camper on the back and that ugly homemade trailer following along behind. We looked just like people straight out of the Great Depression, like all those desperate sojourners had looked while out on the road in their dilapidated old vehicles as they crippled along toward the promise of better living conditions way out in California.

We Johnson kids were terribly embarrassed by this way of traveling. Mortified, really. We knew that it was the late 1950s and the Depression was officially over. The endless string of migrants heading west on the heavily traveled Route 66, or the Mother Road, leading out to the agricultural pickings far away from the Dustbowl had come to an end. The traumatizing circumstances that had compelled these desperate folks to seek greener pastures somewhere out west were supposed to have ended. Our history books in school had clearly depicted, through black and white photographs and crisply written narrative, that this caravan of lost souls *had* come to an end, an end to an American saga, and the literal end, finally, of an extremely painful era in the history of a nation.

But here the Johnsons were, certainly by appearance but by despairing need as well, reliving the very same scenario all over again. While not seeking work in the late summer harvest fields, we were instead simply castaways, a newly homeless family searching for a patch of waterless desert out in Roswell, a place that would hopefully welcome us once again.

Gladys, David, Gloria and I, Johnny, the bedraggled Johnson kids, still bore the dreadful responsibility of selling homemade potholders and aprons from door to door in the small towns along the westward route. Each of us was terribly embarrassed by this form of commerce not unlike the identical feelings of shame we suffered by our mode of travel down the roads.

Indeed, we were completely mortified through and through.

The meager amounts of cash money raised from any sales (twenty-five cents per potholder and seventy-five cents for each apron) were somehow sufficient for keeping the gas tank in the old pickup truck filled. This task was much easier when the filling stations along the highways in Oklahoma and even in Texas were involved in a "gas war" where the advertised cost of one gallon of regular gasoline could be as low as eighteen cents! Even ethyl gasoline required in the big Oldsmobile, Pontiac and Cadillac cars would be priced at only twenty-three cents for each gallon that those thirsty cars would require.

The gas tank in the pickup always took priority over the meager earnings from "potholders and aprons" sales. It had to be constantly refilled, repeatedly, to ever make it all the way back to Roswell.

Another real priority, though, was milk for Geneva's baby bottle. A quart carton of whole milk watered down by little cans of Carnation evaporated milk did the job quite nicely and usually left a few dollars for picking up small tins of canned sardines, packed in a tomato sauce or mustard sauce or just plain oil. A jar of Miracle Whip and a loaf or two of Holsum-brand white bread served to keep the family from starving.

It truly was a dreadful responsibility that we kids had to shoulder, this selling of extremely thin potholders and one-size-fits-all aprons. Maybe it was one thing to perform this function as we traveled east toward paradise in the Ozarks, but driving west once again, heading out to the barren and windswept desert of New Mexico, was of itself disheartening. We allowed no enthusiasm, feigned though it would certainly be, to show on our faces or even in our body language as we went forth in our shabby clothing attempting to peddle Momma's carefully handmade wares to any housewife who would answer the light knock on the front screen door around mid-day and listen to our timid, barely audible voice as we asked:

"Would you like to buy some potholders or aprons?"

We were desperately poor. It showed on levels that covered practically every part of our daily living.

And we had just turned our backs on the Ozarks! We kids couldn't help having severely negative feelings. We simply could not muster the same level of hope for the future that we once had after being forced to participate, all over again, in those humiliating door-to-door sales.

Apparently being smack dab in the middle between my sisters and brother as an eleven-year-old boy in our completely dysfunctional family wasn't enough. Apparently not. I was the only one who suffered from a long-standing speech problem that was most likely at its worst during those stressful times standing at some stranger's front door as I stuttered while asking my feeble salesman's question. What an image and sound that must have presented!

My personal anguish was always heightened when anyone was outside to see me approaching with my large and weathered brown grocery bag with the top rolled down to allow for a handhold grip and filled to overflowing with the merchandise for sale. And no day could be more dreadful for this sales solicitation than when other children my age, particularly boys, were in the yard by the door or in the street in front of their own house.

Those scenarios were terrorizing, forcing me to walk to the opposite side of the street after spying them from afar. Since they were *normal* boys who lived in normal houses and dressed in normal attire—faded Levi jeans and colorful pullover shirts—my personal clothing consisting of wrinkled short-sleeved cotton shirts and elastic-banded pants, both handsewn by my mother, along with my unclean and rather unkept appearance, belied my far less-than-normal station as a young boy in America in 1959. That boyhood was anything but normal; it showed. And I certainly knew it. That debilitating truth was deposited deep inside me, a place that was impossible to reach, somewhere deep down in my soul.

The evasive maneuvers I used to avoid any encounter with those that I felt so entirely inferior to were not always successful.

The most egregious failed attempt at avoidance of those my age happened in a small town called Lone Grove that was probably less than ten miles beyond Ardmore, Oklahoma. It was just before noon on an eastbound street where every house appeared to have a chain-link fence in the front with a small gate that I had to open to walk up to the front door and make my feeble knock and the standard question in my stuttering voice. Already turned away without the sale of even a single potholder at the first three houses, I glanced up the street and saw the four boys leaning up against the fence at a place only two more houses ahead on the same side I was canvassing.

My reaction was swift and deliberate. I immediately crossed the street to begin knocking on doors with every intention of working my way back down the street in the same direction I had started from. That maneuver should work. It just had to work!

The gate at the fence across the street squeaked as I opened it to walk up the sidewalk of the pale-yellow house from which the sound of a country song could be heard through an open door. After my knock, a man answered and threw open the screen door to gain a better look at me. I gave my timid sales pitch, to which he replied that "the missus" wasn't even home, so I would not be able to display any of the potholders or aprons that were stuffed in my brown paper bag. He then pulled the screen door closed and disappeared.

Pivoting to walk back toward the gate, I froze in place when I saw the four guys standing just outside the fence by the gate. They had crossed the street as well and were waiting for me to walk back out onto the sidewalk that ran in front of the houses lining the street. One appeared to be older than the others, most likely already a teenager. Two of them might have been twins; both had matching crewcuts and faint freckles high on their cheekbones. The fourth boy appeared to be exactly my age with curly blond hair and steely blue eyes, eyes that were boring a hole straight through me.

It was the oldest one who spoke, telling the others to clear away from in front of the gate to let me pass through. Knowing that I had no viable choice but to walk that gauntlet on my trembling legs to gain my freedom from them, I hurriedly proceeded through the gate out to the sidewalk with the full intention of turning to my right and getting away in the very same direction that I had initially come from.

Suddenly they closed in around me, preventing any escape. The taunts started immediately:

"Hey, little guy, we saw you down there. Why did you cross the street, huh? Were you afraid of us?"

Snatching my paper sack from my hand, the teenager snarled, "So, let's see what you have in here. Whoa! These look like dresses!" He then draped a couple of the aprons across the top of the fence before us.

"They're my M…M…Momma's aprons. And they're f…for s…s…sale," was my barely audible reply.

One of the twins interjected, "Hey, maybe he should wear one of those dresses or whatever they are," to which his brother roared with laughter, proclaiming, "That's a good idea!"

It was then that the curly-headed boy spoke. He was standing so close to me that I could feel his breath on my neck, and I desperately wanted to get away. Far away.

"So, you're a Momma's boy, ain't ya? And what do we have here, anyway?" He had lifted my hair from the back and continued, "So, did your Momma put a sugar bowl over your head before she cut your hair?"

And then real terror struck like a knife blade straight through my gut when the teenager loudly suggested, "Let's de-pants him!" They all started whooping like coyotes over a downed rabbit as that bully grabbed me and threw me straight down onto the sidewalk. I was frozen by fear but started crying and yelling out for help. Any help from anybody would do. "Please help me!"

Then we all heard the man's loud voice calling from the walkway directly behind us. "Ricky! Now Ricky, you guys leave that boy alone. And get out of here! Get away from my property!"

As the mob took off running, I scrambled to put the aprons and the dropped potholders back into the big, crumpled grocery bag and started off running myself with a quick glance over my shoulder at my rescuer who remained by his screen door watching. And he waved to me as I ran away. I waved back.

I had only made it to the far side of the next yard when I saw the lady standing at her fence. She called out to me, saying that she'd like to buy whatever I was selling. Really? I skidded to a stop and walked over to her, panting, trying to catch my breath.

She took the first apron that I pulled out of the sack, exclaiming her delight with the color scheme of rose and yellow. And she said she just loved the potholder that was right on top of everything else in the bag.

"You just wait right here while I go inside to get my purse. I'll be right back."

Noticing that I had twisted around to check if those boys were still anywhere nearby, she said, "Oh, don't worry about those old bullies. They're long gone and hiding out somewhere. You'll be okay. Now you just wait right here."

After shoving the dollar bill down into the pocket of my trousers, I looked over toward the screen door of my new best friend's house to see him still standing there and waving me off one last time.

I never told anyone about the complete shaming that I had so narrowly escaped. There was no need to ever relive that trauma again. Never, even if it was just in the retelling of the episode. I did tell Momma that it had been a tough day for sales, though, but proudly presented the single, crumpled dollar bill, knowing that it would probably be enough for three cans of sardines for supper.

So, on we went, from one small town to the next. We were inching along on the journey west.

But there was one among us who really couldn't have cared less how we presented to the rest of society. It was Geneva. For her, the whole disruption was just a grand road adventure!

Total defeat was written over everyone's face, from Daddy to Momma to Gladys, and on down through David, me, and Little Sister, too. The only one who remained cheerful, even exuberant and bubbly, was our innocent baby sister, Geneva. By that first week in August of 1959 when we pulled out of Arkansas, she was already twenty-one months old. At that age, she couldn't possibly help herself from being happy all the way around.

8   A ROOFLESS SHANTY

By the middle of August, we had "circled the wagons" on two barren lots out west of Roswell that Daddy had managed to purchase with nothing more than a Promissory Note and an obligation to pay the exact amount of fifteen dollars a month for each one. And by the last week of September in 1959, the following news article appeared in the Roswell Daily Record:

Several organizations and individuals have become interested in a family of seven people living on the outskirts of Roswell. The family is living in a roofless shanty that is entirely unsuitable for cold weather; the husband and father says he is unable to do any heavy work, the wife and mother does housework, sewing, and so on. The man has applied for welfare assistance, but his application—pending a complete physical examination—hasn't even been approved to date. The family, including five children from two to fifteen years of age, came to the attention, first, of a city employee who has been working to assist them, including a possible job with light work for the father, who is in his 60s. Plans are underway, too, to provide the family with an old barracks building for a house, to replace the scrap lumber, roofless shanty before the weather really gets cold. It's somewhat amazing, in this land of plenty, that a family could be in such circumstances, with little food and almost no living quarters. But it happens.

9   NEEFA-DO

The blinding southern New Mexico dust storm had started the previous afternoon around twelve-thirty and had not let up through the entire night, coating everything around with thick layers, even dunes, of sand and plain light brown dirt. By morning a little after first light it had finally stopped, but not before piling tumbleweeds high up into every corner of the makeshift scrap lumber fencing that was arranged to link the pickup camper shell and trailer in a primitive circle. The blackened coffee pot had succumbed to the wind and was found lying on the ground near the fire box in the middle of the roofless compound.

While Momma and Daddy and Geneva had spent the windy night inside the tiny Masonite-sided trailer and Gladys and Little Sister had bedded down inside the homemade camper that sat on the pickup bed, David and I were pretty much relegated to the elements. At least my brother was. He had wrapped himself with an old canvas tarp to escape the blowing dust while sleeping inside the raised rabbit hutch that had been scrounged up by Daddy during one of his runs out to the abandoned old dump site southeast of Roswell. I lucked out by getting to sleep on the bench seat of the less than airtight cab of the old pickup truck.

We had overheard our mother complaining that the water was getting quite low in the old milk can that was filled periodically with fresh water while in town. She had stated that the dipper was now hitting the bottom, and that really worried her. She had scraped up enough to make oatmeal mush for our breakfast, though, but water for drinking and for making supper would take the very last of it. And dirty laundry items were piling up and needed attention soon, especially the cloth diapers that always seemed to be in scarce supply. It was time for Daddy to pull the pickup away from our little compound and head into town with Momma for water and other supplies.

Gladys had seemed especially irritable ever since we had parked out on the vacant lots west of Roswell to set up our very makeshift camp. At fifteen, she didn't usually resist letting her emotions show, either. No doubt she really missed the cushy arrangement she had enjoyed back in the Ozarks. Didn't all of us pine for what we had left behind?

My own heart had been shattered to pieces when we pulled out of Arkansas. Brenda, my beautiful blond-haired girlfriend during my fifth-grade year at Stilwell Elementary School, had expressed a strong desire to continue "going steady" with me when we saw each other once again when school started up in the fall. Unable to see each other even one time during the school break because her entire summer had been spent with her grandparents whose place was down in Hatfield, I had longed for the first day of the sixth grade to start. We would be in the same classroom, and I would see her smiling face again!

There had been no opportunity to say a permanent goodbye. Brenda would return wearing her gorgeous pale blue dress, or maybe that pale yellow one that set off her beautiful eyes and golden hair. She would look around to find me and eventually discover that I was no longer even enrolled anywhere in the Mena Public School system. And her heart would break into a thousand pieces as well.

So, it wasn't just my sister who had lost her perfect arrangement. I had lost my perfect love!

It seemed to me that most of my sister's frustrations were vented only in my direction. Not toward David, who enjoyed being her favorite sibling, probably, nor Gloria, and usually not Geneva. It felt to me like I was so often on the receiving end of most of her irritation and even her anger. But was that really true? Or was it nothing more than a misconception on the part of an eleven-year-old who couldn't understand what it was that I had managed to say or do that seemed to trigger her? It took an observation from Little Sister to understand the dynamics at play between the two of us. She had told me that we both were extremely frustrated about many things and were probably just directing those frustrations at each other. We were provoking each other, apparently. Still, my learning to stay completely under the radar while around her would become mandatory. In fact, it already was. I was already practicing that ducking behavior! But my reprieve was fast approaching since school would be starting in one week.

To steer clear of my older sister as much as possible during the final week before boarding a school bus for the fall, I continued to pour myself into playing with my twenty-one-month-old baby sister, Geneva. That effort was not actually hard, since the toddler was so adorable and fun to be around, and the fun times were addictive for both of us. Always cheerful, unless her bottle feeding was overdue, she delighted in being swung around and around in circles, begging for it to never end. And like any little one, she loved the tickling sessions that usually lasted a long time.

Gloria and David often joined in on the playtimes. He and I would swing the girl back and forth repeatedly between us while Little Sister would crouch down to reach out and tickle her belly as she swung forward. Her cackling laughter was loud and quite contagious as we giggled right along with her.

By the time she had turned three and then four she had started relishing story time. Like every child, she enjoyed fanciful nursery rhymes. She literally craved hearing the stories from the battered but treasured big book of tales for young children. But even much earlier, Geneva had thrilled to our made-up rhymes, like, "Neefa-Do, I love you!"

Interestingly, the name Neefa-Do, which had been coined by her brother David, had stuck, and became, essentially, a nickname. In fact, when she climbed on the school bus to begin her very first day of school, she announced to her seatmate that her name was Neefa-Do Johnson!

(And an entire lifetime later, that same "nickname" continues to be used when her other brother, John, addresses her each birthday with "Happy birthday, Neefa-Do!" How's that for a real nickname sticking around awhile)?

The John Deere backhoe tractor with its trademark green and yellow colors showed up out of the blue one warm Saturday morning in early October. We kids gawked at the driver who had climbed down and asked to speak with our father, but Daddy had heard the tractor as it pulled up and was already heading over to talk with the young operator. Before long, a smooth graded area about seventy feet long and a little over thirty-five feet wide had been carved into the desert floor. In less than two hours the job was finished, and the backhoe was loaded onto the big white truck and hauled away.

After asking Momma what in the world was going on, we all headed over to play on this "foundation" for a house that was already scheduled to be moved onto the scraped-off ground. Everybody agreed that the building would be long and narrow based on the area that had been graded, but no one was ready for the house that came down at an angle from Brown Road pulled by a semi-truck with long trailer rails on which the house was balanced.

It was the next Saturday in October around noontime when the monstrosity rolled onto the lot. The house was incredibly long and extremely narrow with a red tile façade over the front door and the whole front end. Painted a sand-colored brown on stucco with a slightly peaked metal roof, the building looked solid with all the window glass intact and only small cracks showing here and there in the stucco. But overall, it was now abundantly evident for everyone to see that the new Johnson dwelling was significantly different. It was no longer just a roofless shanty!

Knowing that our parents had been entirely unable to contribute monetarily to this new house, we older children reflected on the kindness and generosity of strangers from the town of Roswell. It was clear that the newspaper article must have touched the hearts of many locals who donated very tangible things, like the green-colored butane tank that showed up the next Monday, followed by the tall six by six post that was drilled into position out at the corner of the shed by Southwestern Public Service Electric Company to send power to the house. Finally, we'd have electric lights instead of just lamplight from a kerosene table lamp. We would also now have an electrical outlet on the wall for plugging in a refrigerator!

A couple of used appliances and pieces of furniture were also delivered to our house during the next few weeks, including a gas range and oven in light shades of cream and green, a single-door Philco refrigerator boasting a small freezer section inside, and a divan in green with its spare Scandinavian design that graced the living room so well. And a box of toys suitable for any two-year-old girl had also arrived, with a ten-inch plastic baby doll found inside that was dressed in a bright red pajama outfit. Geneva had quickly fallen in love with the doll and had soon given her the name of Betty-Baby.

Now, at long last, all members of the Johnson family would have warm sleeping quarters *inside* our sixty-foot-long house rather than outside under olive drab tarps to stave off the freezing rain or hide from falling snow during the winter nights.

The building itself was nothing more than a former tavern that had originally served all the menfolk who worked in the cotton gin in downtown Roswell close to Third Street and Main adjacent to the old railroad tracks. While its historical function was noteworthy, the place was like paradise to us. Who cared that it once had little cocktail tables in both the front room and in the overflow space in the next room, the one with the wide arched entry and two built-in wooden seats that folded down out of the wall over in the corner behind what had been the narrow portable bar? And who really cared all that much that it no longer supported an inside restroom located down the hall like it once had? At least the structure had wooden floors, plastered and painted walls, glassed-in windowpanes, and a tin roof. A roof!

A strong commitment to replace our roofless shanty had been met with this wonderful donation from the townsfolk of the southeastern New Mexico town of Roswell, the place we would continue to call home for the next decade and a half, until each child had either graduated from high school and left for college or married and moved off to Texas. Yes! Roswell was now our long-term home.

The green Mercury station wagon barreled into the yard enshrouded in a cloud of fine dust and came to a stop only after the front wheels rested in the slight gulley at the extreme southeast corner of the yard some twenty feet from the front porch where I was seated. The occupants of the car could be heard in loud off-key singing even before the doors popped open. Out spilled all eight children, every one under the age of twelve by all appearances, followed by the three-hundred-pound driver who was still bellowing out the lyrics to "Joy Unspeakable and Full of Glory" as his wife sang along.

We were not expecting the Matthews to come for a visit, and certainly not right around suppertime. That clan must have been hungry to invite themselves for a meal just as the panned batter bread was coming out of the oven! And how had they figured out which place was ours? There was no address number on the house. There wasn't even a street marker of any sort anywhere around!

Yet they somehow managed to show up right at five o'clock on that Monday evening in July. We scarcely even knew who they were, but there they were, all ten of them!

Daddy had remained outside in the shade seated on the old free-standing car seat where he and Momma would sit to escape the summer heat trapped inside the house. Momma had already gone back into the kitchen to scare up something for our supper before he noticed the dust floating by up at the front of the house. He then witnessed the enormously long, low car come to an abrupt stop right at the shallow ditch.

He quickly rose to hurry over to investigate who had just arrived, uninvited and unannounced, in our yard out in the country. He discovered that each occupant from the station wagon was now standing around in the dirt of the front yard with the kids talking away, with one of the young girls asking, "I wonder what's for supper around this house?" Their father was still exercising his vocal cords with the same refrain about unspeakable joy, but at least at a considerably lower volume.

And what a break for me that Daddy had walked up to greet our visitors as quickly as he had, allowing me to almost immediately bolt through the front door and hurry through the house to tell my brother and sisters that we had company. I then breathlessly told Momma about the people outside and that we had company to feed for supper as well, since I had heard the young girl's general yet giveaway question just before entering the house.

Through gritted teeth, Momma implored, "Who *are* they? How dare they just barge in here at suppertime and expect us to be able to feed them and us too!"

"It's that big family from church, the new ones that just moved here from Mississippi. You know them— that preacher named Brother Matthews," I replied.

"He showed up here with Sister Matthews, too, and all their family. I'm pretty sure I counted at least eight kids in all."

David and Geneva had gone outside to stand on the porch to get a good look at all the visitors, but Gladys and Gloria had entered the kitchen just as Momma's attitude had abruptly changed as evidenced by her announcement that we would just "do the best with what we've got."

What a remarkable, instantaneous change!

She then instructed the girls to quickly open two cans of creamed corn and start warming the contents over a burner with some added water to stretch out the helpings. She reached for the last twenty-nine ounce can of delicious, shredded beef in rich brown gravy from the shelf that held our nonperishable surplus commodities issued to needy families by the federal government.

The job she gave me was to immediately find enough salvaged desserts that we had rescued from the huge paper sacks that had been discarded behind both the Piggly Wiggly and Furr's grocery stores downtown. I managed to place enough Danish pastries, with one half of them blueberry and the other apricot, on a plate that could satisfy everyone's sweet tooth while making absolutely sure that not a single one had any trace of current or previously pinched off blue mold.

Hospitality. Forced hospitality at that. We had "killed the fatted calf" for our company and the meal and visitation had gone well enough that evening. All the younger children played outside until it got dark, but inside the talk had been cordial if not a little one-sided and seemingly endless. Kevin Matthews held sway with tales of the family's endless adventures way down south on the Gulf, making me wonder why he had chosen to drag his family away from that part of the country to the completely foreign wasteland of southeastern New Mexico, to the so-called Land of Enchantment which really wasn't enchanted at all.

I also wondered at his preaching. We had listened to the loud and rather emotional delivery of three of his messages on Sunday nights. They had all been a bit long-winded but loaded with scripture that he had memorized! He did lug around a huge leather-bound Thompson Chain-Reference Bible in the King James version, but he seldom read directly from it because he knew from memory the passages on the opened pages. Unbelievable!

By his own admission, he had not attended any Bible College, let alone any formal Seminary, claiming such attendance was unnecessary for a person to preach the Gospel. How evident that was!

So, as an opinionated, know-it-all young teenager at thirteen, I had determined that Reverend Matthews was a dynamic messenger of the Word, regardless of whether he was really only a mama-called preacher or a genuine, bona fide, God-called one!

To be very sure, the call from the Ozarks never totally ceased from its magnetic tug on Momma and Daddy, but there would not be another pulling up of stakes and leaving New Mexico behind again. Neither would the call from the Ozarks continue to be an exclusive claim on them, since Arizona had also started calling.

They would manage to patch together enough cash money to drive the old pickup back to Missouri and camp for one week out in Clark's barn on their forty acres in the Racine area. Those short trips would take place practically every summer, always in the month of June. But despite the new pull out to the saguaro-dotted landscape of Arizona, those sojourns back to Missouri survived for a least a couple more years.

They would naturally take Geneva and the rest of us kids with them down to the Ozarks. The trips were a wonderful respite from the endless boredom out on the desolate, windblown desert of New Mexico.

How fortuitous for Neefa-Do during the summer of 1963 when our baby sister was six and one-half years old. She would experience her very first love! His name was Mark Clark, and he was nine. With curly brown hair and lady-killer good looks, he had swept Geneva right off her feet. He had been solicitous of her during the entire week, offering a combination of perfect manners and genuine kindness toward her that had completely knit her heart to him. And Mark knew he had won Geneva all for himself. This young love was pure and genuine and beautiful to behold!

Time often takes a real toll on young love, just as it did with this sweet New Mexico girl and the boy from the Ozarks. As it turned out, Geneva and Mark never saw each other again because our parents, Gene and Harleigh Johnson, had now fully transitioned to only traveling west to the warmer climate out in Phoenix. That is exactly what they had done the previous year, spending the entire summer in that broiling heat.

In that summer of 1962, the whole family except for Gladys, who had already married and was living in Amarillo with her husband Deon, had moved into a two-bedroom weekly rental situated directly behind old Mr. Rutkowski's enormous used furniture store, where we remained throughout the balance of June, the entire month of July, but only the first half of August.

School was about to start up once again in Roswell. Since we had retained our converted tavern out at Auto Route West, we were quickly ready to board the school bus on Monday for the beginning of the fall semester in the Roswell Independent School District.

During our summer absence while the premises had been vacant, there had been no break-ins, leaving our few pieces of furniture and our winter clothing undisturbed. Even the blue transistor radio stashed up on a high shelf was still in its place, signifying that the only loose item that might have had any value at all had not been removed.

So, while it appeared that no one had broken into the house to steal anything, there *had* been an intrusion. Oh, yes! The very first evidence of this violation was when Gloria noticed the large brown tarantula scurry away toward her bedstead to hide beneath the bare mattress. Gloria had immediately let loose a blood-curdling scream at the sighting which caused Geneva to join her in the hysteria that lasted until the spider was removed from the house by offering the end of a long broom handle to crawl onto.

And Momma had spotted clear evidence over on the kitchen countertop of something as well. It had been a full-force invasion of mice! From the look of things, all those filthy rodents had just moved right in!

Those nasty discoveries were a reminder of the time, years earlier at the old one-room place, when Daddy had discovered something utterly gruesome when he was drawing up water from the cistern. Lying at the bottom of the underground concrete-lined tank was a dead vinegarroon with the long whip tail stretched out behind the body. When he announced the find, we all gathered around to peer over the edge of the cistern to view the ugly monster that had drowned. And after Momma had seen the dead scorpion, she assured us that any lingering vinegar acid that had potentially spewed from the tail during the throes of drowning would be diluted by the vast reservoir of water so there wouldn't be the slightest detectable difference in the taste of our drinking water. We all earnestly hoped that she was right!

The return trip to New Mexico had been seamless, completely unlike the infamous outbound journey in June when we pulled away from Roswell on our way out to Arizona—a journey that we kids had come to remember as the Salt River Canyon Odyssey.

The trip had been routine at the start. Actually, it had been much better than just routine, since the chosen westward route had taken us through the mountains to Capitan and Carrizozo before continuing west on U.S. 60 toward the small village of Magdalena, where we had pulled off the highway to set up camp for the night. Pie Town, a tiny community that had boasted a small bakery in the early 1920s that specialized in apple pies, would be reached the following morning before crossing into the mountains of Arizona and driving past the towns of Springerville and Show Low.

When it was time, by early afternoon, to stop for a rest and, more importantly, to give the overheating radiator a rest, we took the wide turnoff at the crest of a long hill northeast of Globe where the Salt River churned through a canyon floored by broad granite rocks where rushing water formed small waterfalls and pools.

The radiator in the old truck was in desperate need of a rest. In fact, the steam escaping all around the hood indicated that it was suffering from a major boil-over! Daddy had not needed to switch the key to the off position since the engine had already frozen up and shut down completely. When he attempted to raise the hood, he was turned back by the scalding steam. That hood raising would simply have to wait. It would take some time for everything to finally cool down enough to activate the lever to open things up.

My brother and sisters were just as thrilled as I was to have ample time for exploring down by the river. The descent was made easy by an established but steep path that ended right at the water's edge. We stayed right on the bank to watch the swirling water, since it was flowing much too rapidly and appeared to be deep in certain places. Besides, not one of us could even swim, so any entrance into the water or slippage off the huge granite slabs surrounded by the twisting, dancing water would have no doubt proven to be disastrous.

We noticed that Daddy had stood or walked along the edge of the pullout above us. It wasn't difficult to figure out that he was there to keep an eye on us. His intention was to prevent us from voluntarily stepping into the water or climbing on the wet rocks.

The raging river fascinated each of us as we ambled along on the damp eastern bank. And we delighted in drops of water that regularly managed to escape the general flow to bounce up onto our skin. What a fabulous cooling touch on such a hot day!

When Daddy finally waved us back up to where he was waiting near the pickup, we hurried up the path, pausing at the top for a turn-around and a final look at the roaring water as it crashed over the rocks on a journey down through the canyon on the way to the Valley of the Sun.

After we had climbed back inside the covered pickup bed and settled into our customary seating areas, we heard the fruitless effort coming from the starter. It was refusing to catch to get the motor started. The continued turning was already starting to slow, since the battery was clearly fading and would not be able to hold out for too much more grinding.

When the cab door opened, Daddy stepped out and came around to the back and told us to get out.

"The engine got too hot. We'll need to give this truck a push. Momma will help. Now Geneva, you just stay up on that bed."

Our mother pushed from a middle position between Gloria and David while my spot was out on the right end. After Daddy had returned to the cab and seated himself behind the wheel, he called out to us to start pushing. Straining against the tailgate with every bit of strength we could muster, we leaned into the job, but it scarcely got the vehicle to roll. It was then that our father jumped out and started helping from the opened driver's door. That effort proved crucial, and the truck started rolling! But when he jumped back inside the cab, all that forward momentum slowed considerably. We knew that we'd now need to push so much harder and redoubled our efforts.

We pushed with all our strength and pushed some more! Finally, the truck was rolling along, but that jerking attempt at starting the motor by popping the clutch had failed and some speed had been lost. So, we kept pushing, hoping that the second attempt at forcing a start would work.

But now something was more than a little different. We were now rolling slightly downhill, and the speed had picked up dramatically. There was no longer any need for more pushing since we were now literally running with the truck. It was time to let go!

It was then that tragedy struck. Momma stumbled as she let go of her grip on the tailgate, falling face down onto the pavement and onto a jagged quarter-sized rock that just missed connecting with her right eye. We kids braked our running and whirled back around to assist her. Since she was considerably overweight, David and I were unable to even get her into a sitting position. She had managed to raise her head up from the pavement to reveal blood flowing profusely back down to the asphalt.

Geneva was screaming in terror at the image, rapidly receding, of her own mother lying face down on the pavement under the hot sun. Gloria was loudly crying while cradling Momma's head. And David, always an incredibly fast runner, had hauled away chasing the now-motorized pickup to let Daddy know what had happened. But the vehicle was already backing up to join the scene of the highway carnage.

Momma's bandana had slipped off her head when she had fallen and was lying nearby. Daddy grabbed it and immediately placed it as a pressure bandage over the bleeding wound, a deep gash appearing on the forehead just above the right eyebrow. He then maneuvered the bandana, which was still knotted, into place on her head with it resting just above both eyebrows instead of up at the top of her forehead.

David and I assisted him as he picked his sobbing wife up from the road and guided her into the cab, where Gloria cleaned the blood off her face and neck.

Momma received no professional medical attention that afternoon nor on any other day that followed. The improvised bandage had effectively worked to stop the hemorrhaging, and our crossed fingers and prayers would simply have to be enough to prevent any nasty infection from setting in.

The scar on her forehead would forever be worn as a badge that would remain visible the rest of her days.

Tragedy had struck that day at Salt River Canyon in Arizona—a huge tragedy for our mother. Witnessing the accident had been traumatic for young Neefa-Do. It had been for the rest of us, too.

And no one ever wanted to remember that horrible episode as the Salt River Canyon Odyssey, either. But we all did.

There were still the everlasting Ozarks—the rolling green hills with occasional bubbling springs evident right alongside the road at the pull-off, or a thread-like waterfall slipping right down onto the highway shoulder on a hilltop near Seneca where a tiny shop attached to a Gulf filling station offered shortbread cookies studded with chopped black walnuts.

There were still the sounds down in the Ozarks—the daytime music from warblers coupled with unending nocturnal choruses from cicadas and the loud calling of toads and the croaking of frogs from a hundred scattered ponds and creeks all around.

There were still the natives of the Ozarks—the many good-hearted folks who populated all the towns and the countryside in that part of America, some who were enduring friends, like the Clarks of Racine, who tended to always treat the Johnsons just like family with genuine warmth and kindness and helpfulness.

There were still the losses from the Ozarks—the 1959 heartbreak for an 11-year-old boy who would never again see his blond-haired Brenda and the vanishing of a summer love affair between a 6-year-old girl and a 9-year-old boy.

No. Neefa-Do would never again see her boyfriend from the Missouri Ozarks.

Mark was completely lost to her now, but she would still forever cherish the memories of that sweet love from the summer of 1963. Nothing, indeed no one person, ever, would be able to take those precious memories away!

EPILOGUE

The new, still untagged California van with the darkly tinted windows all around slowly crawled along on the roads out west of Roswell, five miles out in the rural area that had been known only as Auto Route West during the 1950s and 1960s.

It was a late July evening with the sun about a half-hour from setting, making it difficult for the driver to see much in the way of detail when looking through dark sunglasses into the sun. Properties on the east side of each roadway were all fully illuminated by the waning sunlight, though, so the work was made easy while viewing in that direction.

A diligent effort was underway to locate one specific small house that would likely be accessed by one of the many dirt roads that still dominated most of the area even seventy years later. Operating strictly from distant memories of that long ago time, the driver, John, had already slowly driven past each place and had even traveled on the three paved streets in the area. I knew the location where the house should be, generally, assuming it was still standing after these many decades. But that road was blacktopped, and the place had two wide mobile homes inside a large pipe-fenced yard with massive, evenly spaced shade trees totally circling the double lots, so it just couldn't be the proper street for pinpointing the place, which would likely resemble nothing more than a broken-down shack after all the time that had passed. But a paved street? Mobile homes? No. How was that even possible?

I became anxious when a pickup started driving along behind me, feeling certain that the driver might be functioning as a de facto enforcer for a neighborhood watch program. When I found a spot to pull over, the blue truck initially slowed considerably before finally moving around my vehicle. "That was a close one," I thought as I guessed that the driver had been the old man looking out of his kitchen window at me when I had earlier stopped in front of his place and lowered my window to get a clearer view of his entire house while looking directly into the sun. Could it be the house I was looking for? Moving on, I had circled back and examined the house from a stopped position yet another time, but this time left the window rolled up.

Many things about that particular house seemed to fit the place my father had built back in 1953, but of critical importance was the lack of a doorway in the appropriate place on the northeast corner and the absence of a window where it should have been and, most telling, the stovepipe chimney definitely being in the wrong location.

The slanting sunlight would disappear in only a few short minutes. This search had ended up being futile, and I had resigned to just call it quits and head into town to my hotel for the night.

Since I was still in the immediate vicinity of where I was almost certain the old house should have been, I turned south on the paved road that went past the west side of that tree-ringed double lot that would take me down to Hendricks Street and then west to Brown Road and then a right turn to the north to join the West Second highway back into town.

I wasn't driving all that slowly anymore. It was now dinnertime, and I knew exactly where my preferred restaurant was located up at the top of Main Street. That upcoming meal was my clear focus now, so I was lucky to even be looking between the trees and pipe fencing over on my left.

"What was that?" Could it possibly be *the* house, the little shack that the very last rays of sunlight were shining on?

Hitting the brakes, I slammed the vehicle into reverse and started sliding backwards until the little peek-a-boo view reappeared through my lowered window.

And there it was!

The old structure was now without window glass or any doorway that still closed, and it was surrounded by fencing made of a double strand of chicken wire. A flock of white leghorn chickens was making its way into the shack to begin a long nighttime of roosting.

Chickens—living in our house that Daddy had built in 1953 and the very house in which Geneva was born in 1957!

Borrowing a phrase from my father, Gene Johnson, I let out a loud "Well, great day in the morning!"

And at least in 2022 terms, my baby sister, Geneva, *had* been born in a chicken coop after all!

www.ingramcontent.com/pod-product-compliance
Lightning Source LLC
Chambersburg PA
CBHW051322120626
46547CB00015B/2353